Outside D0391106

Eavan Boland's Carcanet books include
The Journey
Selected Poems

OUTSIDE HISTORY,
Eavan Boland

WITHDRAWN

CARCANET

First published in 1990 by
Carcanet Press Limited
4th Floor, Conavon Court
12-16 Blackfriars Street
Manchester M3 5BQ

British Library Cataloguing in Publication Data
Boland, Eavan, *1944-*
  Outside history.
  I. Title
  823.914 [F]

  ISBN 0-85635-899-1

The publisher acknowledges financial assistance from
the Arts Council of Great Britain.

Set in 11pt Palatino by Bryan Williamson, Darwen, Lancashire
Printed in England by SRP Ltd., Exeter

For Kevin Casey

Acknowledgements

Thanks are due to the editors of the following publications in which these poems, sometimes in different forms, first appeared:

The Atlantic Monthly: 'The Achill Woman'; 'The Latin Lesson'
The Yale Review: 'The Shadow Doll'
Ploughshares: 'The Rooms of Other Women Poets'
Antaeus: 'On the Gift of "The Birds of America" by
    John James Audubon'
Pequod: 'The Photograph on my Father's Desk'
New Yorker: 'The Black Lace Fan my Mother Gave me;
    'Mountain Time'; 'Spring at the Edge of the Sonnet';
    'White Hawthorn in the West of Ireland'; 'The River';
    'What We Lost'; 'Our Origins are in the Sea'; 'Nights of
    Childhood'; 'Midnight Flowers'; 'Distances'.
Triquarterly: 'The Rooms of Other Women Poets';
    'Outside History'

The sequence 'Outside History' appeared in *PN Review* and in *The American Poetry Review*.

'The Achill Woman' and 'Spring at the Edge of the Sonnet' appeared in the *Poetry Book Society Selections* for 1988 and 1989.

'What Love Intended' appeared in *Soho Square* (Bloomsbury 1988).

'The Black Lace Fan my Mother Gave me' appeared in *Last and Always* (Faber 1988).

Thanks are also due to *The Irish Times, The Sunday Tribune, The New Nation, Gown, The Sunday Times, Poetry Review, Poetry Ireland, Oxford Poetry, Krino, Quarry, Poetry Canada* and *Orbis*; BBC 2 (television), BBC 3 (radio); RTE (television and radio), BBC Radio 4 ('Woman's Hour').

I should like to thank Denis and Teresa Cusack, in whose antique shop I saw the Shadow Doll, and who explained its origin to me.

Contents

I: *Object Lessons*

II: *Outside History: a sequence*

III: *Distances*

I

Object Lessons

The Black Lace Fan my Mother Gave me

It was the first gift he ever gave her,
buying it for five francs in the Galeries
in pre-war Paris. It was stifling.
A starless drought made the nights stormy.

They stayed in the city for the summer.
They met in cafés. She was always early.
He was late. That evening he was later.
They wrapped the fan. He looked at his watch.

She looked down the Boulevard des Capucines.
She ordered more coffee. She stood up.
The streets were emptying. The heat was killing.
She thought the distance smelled of rain and lightning.

These are wild roses, appliqued on silk by hand,
darkly picked, stitched boldly, quickly.
The rest is tortoiseshell and has the reticent,
clear patience of its element. It is

a worn-out, underwater bullion and it keeps,
even now, an inference of its violation.
The lace is overcast as if the weather
it opened for and offset had entered it.

The past is an empty café terrace.
An airless dusk before thunder. A man running.
And no way now to know what happened then –
none at all – unless, of course, you improvise:

The blackbird on this first sultry morning,
in summer, finding buds, worms, fruit,
feels the heat. Suddenly she puts out her wing –
the whole, full, flirtatious span of it.

The Rooms of Other Women Poets

I wonder about you: whether the blue abrasions
of daylight, falling as dusk across your page,

make you reach for the lamp. I sometimes think
I see that gesture in the way you use language.

And whether you think, as I do, that wild flowers
dried and fired on the ironstone rim of

the saucer underneath your cup, are a sign of
a savage, old calligraphy: you will not have it.

The chair you use, for instance, may be cane
soaked and curled in spirals, painted white

and eloquent, or iron mesh and the table
a horizon of its own on plain, deal trestles,

bearing up unmarked, steel-cut foolscap,
a whole quire of it; when you leave I know

you look at them and you love their air of
unaggressive silence as you close the door.

The early summer, its covenant, its grace,
is everywhere: even shadows have leaves.

Somewhere you are writing or have written in
a room you came to as I come to this

room with honeyed corners, the interior sunless,
the windows shut but clear so I can see

the bay windbreak, the laburnum hang fire, feel
the ache of things ending in the jasmine darkening early.

Object Lessons

It was yours.
  Your coffee mug. Black,
with a hunting scene on the side
(cruel theatre as the kettle poured).
  Together, we unpacked it
    in the new house.

  A hunting scene:
  Dogs. Hawking. Silk.
Linen spread out in a meadow.
Pitchers of wine clouding in the shadow
  of beech trees. Buttermilk.
    A huntsman.

  A wild rabbit.
  A thrush ready to sing.
A lady smiling as the huntsman kissed her:
the way land looks before disaster
  strikes or suffering
    becomes a habit

    was not a feature
    of the history we knew. Now
it opened out before us, bright
as our curtainless October nights
  whose street-lit glow
    was second nature. Or

  those mornings
  we drank coffee
and shared cake in a kitchen full of
chaos, before we knew the details of
  this pastoral were merely
    veiled warnings

of the shiver
of presentiment with which
we found the broken pieces of
the sparrow hawk and the kisses of
the huntsman, the pitcher
and the thrush's never

to-be-finished
aria, an untouched meal,
and the lady and the hunting horn
on the floorboards you and I had sworn
to sand down and seal
with varnish.

On the Gift of 'The Birds of America'
by John James Audubon

What you have given me is, of course, elegy: the red-shouldered
hawk in among these scattering partridges,
flustered at

such a descent, and the broad-winged one poised on the branch
of a pignut, and the pine siskin and the wren are
an inference

we follow in the plummet of the tern which appears to be,
from this angle anyway, impossibly fragile and
if we imagine

the franchise of light these camphor-coloured wings opened out
once with and are at such a loss for now,
then surely this

is the nature and effect of elegy: the celebration of an element
which absence has revealed: it is
our earthliness

we love as we look at them, which we fear to lose, which we need
this re-phrasing of the air,
of the ocean

to remind us of: that evening, late in May, the Clare hills were
ghostly with hawthorn. Two swans flew over us.
I can still hear

the musical insistence of their wings as they came in past
the treetops, near the lake; and we looked up,
rooted to the spot.

The Game

Outside my window an English spring was
summoning home its birds and a week-long fog
was tattering into wisps and rags and at last
I could see the railings when I looked out.

I was a child in a north-facing bedroom in
a strange country. I lay awake listening to
quarrelling and taffeta creaking and the clattering
of queens and aces on the inlaid card table.

I played a game: I hid my face in the pillow
and put my arms around it until they thickened.
Then I was following the thaw northward and the air
was blonde with frost and sunshine and below me

was only water and the shadow of flight in it
and the shape of wings under it, and in the hours
before morning I would be drawn down and drawn
down and there would be no ground under me

and no safe landing in the dawn breaking on
a room with sharp corners and surfaces on which
the red-jacketed and cruel-eyed fractions of chance
lay scattered where the players had abandoned them.

Later on I would get up and go to school in
the scalded light which fog leaves behind it;
and pray for the King in chapel and feel dumbly for
the archangels trapped in their granite hosannahs.

The Shadow Doll

(This was sent to the bride-to-be in Victorian times,
by her dressmaker. It consisted in a porcelain doll,
under a dome of glass, modelling the proposed
wedding dress.)

They stitched blooms from ivory tulle
to hem the oyster gleam of the veil.
They made hoops for the crinoline.

Now, in summary and neatly sewn –
a porcelain bride in an airless glamour –
the shadow doll survives its occasion.

Under glass, under wraps, it stays
even now, after all, discreet about
visits, fevers, quickenings and lusts

and just how, when she looked at
the shell-tone spray of seed pearls,
the bisque features, she could see herself

inside it all, holding less than real
stephanotis, rose petals, never feeling
satin rise and fall with the vows

I kept repeating on the night before –
astray among the cards and wedding gifts –
the coffee pots and the clocks and

the battered tan case full of cotton
lace and tissue-paper, pressing down, then
pressing down again. And then, locks.

The River

You brought me
    to the mouth of a river
in mid-October
    when the swamp maples
were saw-toothed and blemished.
    I remember

how strange it felt –
    not having any
names for the red oak
    and the rail
and the slantways plunge
    of the osprey.

What we said was less
    than what we saw.
What we saw was
    a duck boat, slowly
passing us, a hunter and
    his spaniel, and

his gun poised,
    and, in the distance,
the tips of the wild
    rice drowning in
that blue which raids and
    excludes light.

Mountain Time

Time is shadowless there: mornings re-occur
only as enchantments, only as time for her

to watch berries ripen by on the mountain ash;
for him, at a short distance from her, to catch fish.

Afterwards, darkness will be only what is left of
a mouth after kissing or a hand laced in a hand;

a branch; a river; will be what is lost of words
as they turn to silences and then to sleep. Yet

when they leave the mountain what he will remember is
the rowan trees: that blemish, that scarlet. She will think of

the arc of the salmon after sudden capture –
its glitter a larceny of daylight on slate.

The Latin Lesson

Easter light in the convent garden.
The eucalyptus tree glitters in it.
A bell rings for
the first class.

Today the Sixth Book of the Aeneid.
An old nun calls down the corridor.
Manners, girls. Where
are your manners?

Last night in his Lenten talk
the local priest asked us to remember
everything is put here
for a purpose:

even eucalyptus leaves are suitable
for making oil from to steep wool in,
to sweeten our blankets
and gaberdines.

My forefinger crawls on the lines.
A storm light comes in from the bay.
How beautiful the words
look, how

vagrant and strange on the page
before we crush them for their fragrance
and crush them again
to discover

the pathway to hell and that these
shadows in their shadow-bodies,
chittering and mobbing
on the far

shore, signalling their hunger for
the small usefulness of a life, are
       the dead. And how
       before the bell

will I hail the black keel and flatter the dark
boatman and cross the river and still
       keep a civil tongue
       in my head?

Bright-Cut Irish Silver

I take it down
from time to time, to feel
the smooth path of silver meet the cicatrice of skill.

These scars, I tell myself, are learned.

This gift for wounding an artery of rock
was passed on from father to son, to the father
of the next son;

is an aptitude
for injuring earth while inferring it in curves and surfaces;

is this cold potency which has come,
by time and chance,

into my hands.

We Were Neutral in the War

This warm, late summer there is so much
to get in. The ladder waits by the crab apple tree.
The greenhouse is rank with the best
Irish tomatoes. Pears are ripening.

Your husband frowns at dinner, has no time
for the baby who has learned to crease three
fingers and wave "day-day". This is serious,
he says. This could be what we all feared.

You pierce a sequin with a needle.
You slide it down single-knotted thread
until it lies with all the others in
a puzzle of brightness. Then another and another one.

Let the green and amber marrows rise up
and beat against it and the crab apples and
the damson-coloured pram by the back
wall: you will not sew them into it.

The wooden ledge of the conservatory
faces south. Row on row,
the pears are laid out there, are hard
and then yellow and then yellow with

a rosiness. You leave them out of it.
They will grow soft and bruised at the top
and rot, all in one afternoon. The light,
which made them startling, you will use.

On the breakfast table the headlines are
telling of a city under threat where
you mixed cheese with bitter fennel and
fell in love over demitasse. Afterwards,

you walked by the moonlit river and stopped
and looked down. A glamorous circumference is
spinning on your needle, is
that moon in satin water making

the same peremptory demands on
the waves of the Irish sea and as each
salt-window opens to reveal
a weather of agates, you will stitch that in

with the orchard colours of the first preserves
you make from the garden. You move the jars from
the pantry to the windowsill where
you can see them: winter jewels.

The night he comes to tell you this is war
you wait for him to put on his dinner jacket.
The party is tonight.
The streets are quiet. Dublin is at peace.

The talk is of death but you take
the hand of the first man who asks you.
You dance the fox-trot, the two-step,
the quick-step,

in time to the music. Exclusions
glitter at your hips and past and future are
the fended-off and far-fetched
in waltz time below your waist.

II

Outside History
A sequence

I

The Achill Woman

She came up the hill carrying water.
She wore a half-buttoned, wool cardigan,
a tea-towel round her waist.

She pushed the hair out of her eyes with
her free hand and put the bucket down.

The zinc-music of the handle on the rim
tuned the evening. An Easter moon rose.
In the next-door field a stream was
a fluid sunset; and then, stars.

I remember the cold rosiness of her hands.
She bent down and blew on them like broth.
And round her waist, on a white background,
in coarse, woven letters, the words 'glass cloth'.

And she was nearly finished for the day.
And I was all talk, raw from college –
week-ending at a friend's cottage
with one suitcase and the set text
of the Court poets of the Silver Age.

We stayed putting down time until
the evening turned cold without warning.
She said goodnight and started down the hill.

The grass changed from lavender to black.
The trees turned back to cold outlines.
You could taste frost

but nothing now can change the way I went
indoors, chilled by the wind
and made a fire
and took down my book
and opened it and failed to comprehend

the harmonies of servitude,
the grace music gives to flattery
and language borrows from ambition –

and how I fell asleep
oblivious to

the planets clouding over in the skies,
the slow decline of the Spring moon,
the songs crying out their ironies.

II

A False Spring

Alders are tasselled.
Flag-iris is already out on the canal.

From my window I can see
the College gardens, crocuses stammering
in pools of rain, plum blossom
on the branches.

I want to find her,
the woman I once was,
who came out of that reading-room
in a hard January, after studying
Aeneas in the underworld,

how his old battle-foes spotted him there –

how they called and called and called
only to have it be
a yell of shadows, an O vanishing in
the polished waters
and the topsy-turvy seasons of hell –

her mind so frail her body was its ghost.

I want to tell her she can rest,
she is embodied now.

But narcissi,
opening too early,
are all I find.
I hear the bad sound of these South winds,
the rain coming from some region which has lost sight
of our futures, leaving us
nothing to look forward to except
what one serious frost can accomplish.

III

The Making of an Irish Goddess

Ceres went to hell
with no sense of time.

When she looked back
all that she could see was

the arteries of silver in the rock,
the diligence of rivers always at one level,
wheat at one height,
leaves of a single colour,
the same distance in the usual light;

a seasonless, unscarred earth.

But I need time –
my flesh and that history –
to make the same descent.

In my body,
neither young now nor fertile,
and with the marks of childbirth
still on it,

in my gestures –
the way I pin my hair to hide
the stitched, healed blemish of a scar –
must be

an accurate inscription
of that agony:

the failed harvests,
the fields rotting to the horizon,
the children devoured by their mothers
whose souls, they would have said,
went straight to hell,
followed by their own.

There is no other way:

myth is the wound we leave
in the time we have –

which in my case is this
March evening
at the foothills of the Dublin mountains,
across which the lights have changed all day,

holding up my hand
sickle-shaped, to my eyes
to pick out
my own daughter from
all the other children in the distance;

her back turned to me.

IV

White Hawthorn in the West of Ireland

I drove West
in the season between seasons.
I left behind suburban gardens.
Lawnmowers. Small talk.

Under low skies, past splashes of coltsfoot,
I assumed
the hard shyness of Atlantic light
and the superstitious aura of hawthorn.

All I wanted then was to fill my arms with
sharp flowers,
to seem, from a distance, to be part of
that ivory, downhill rush. But I knew,

I had always known
the custom was
not to touch hawthorn.
Not to bring it indoors for the sake of

the luck
such constraint would forfeit –
a child might die, perhaps, or an unexplained
fever speckle heifers. So I left it

stirring on those hills
with a fluency
only water has. And, like water, able
to re-define land. And free to seem to be –

for anglers,
and for travellers astray in
the unmarked lights of a May dusk –
the only language spoken in those parts.

V

Daphne Heard with Horror the Addresses of the God

It was early summer. Already
the conservatory was all steam and greenness.
I would have known the stephanotis by
its cut-throat sweetness anywhere.
We drank tea. You were telling me
a story you had heard as a child,
about the wedding of a local girl,
long ago, and a merchant from Argyll.

I thought the garden looked so at ease.
The roses were beginning on one side.
The laurel hedge was nothing but itself,
and all of it so free of any need
for nymphs, goddesses, wounded presences –
the fleet river-daughters who took root
and can be seen in the woods in
unmistakable shapes of weeping.

You were still speaking. By the time
I paid attention they were well married:
the bridegroom had his bride on the ship.
The sails were ready to be set. You said
small craft went with her to the ship and,
as it sailed out, well-wishers
took in armfuls, handfuls, from the boats
white roses and threw them on the water.

We cleared up then, saying how
the greenfly needed spraying, the azaleas
were over; and you went inside. I
stayed in the heat looking out at
the garden in its last definition.
Freshening and stirring. A suggestion,
behind it all, of darkness. In the shadow,
beside the laurel hedge, its gesture.

VI

The Photograph on my Father's Desk

It could be
any summer afternoon.

The sun is warm on
the fruitwood garden seat.
Fuchsia droops.
Thrushes move to get
windfalls underneath the crab apple tree.

The woman
holds her throat like a wound.

She wears
mutton-coloured gaberdine with
a scum of lace
just above her boot

which is pointed at
this man coming down the path with
his arms wide open. Laughing.

The garden fills up
with a burned silence.

The talk has stopped.
The spoon which just now
jingled at the rim of the lemonade jug
is still.

And the shrubbed lavender
will find
neither fragrance nor muslin.

VII

We are Human History.
We are not Natural History.

At twilight in
the shadow of the poplars
the children found a swarm of wild bees.

It was late summer and I knew as
they came shouting in that, yes,
this evening had been singled out by

a finger pointing at trees,
the inland feel of that greenness,
the sugar-barley iron of a garden chair

and children still bramble-height
and fretful from the heat and a final
brightness stickle-backing that particular

patch of grass across which light
was short-lived and elegiac as
the view from a train window of

a station parting, all tears. And this –
this I thought, is how it will have been
chosen from those summer evenings

which under the leaves of the poplars –
striped dun and ochre, simmering over
the stashed-up debris of old seasons –

a swarm of wild bees is making use of.

VIII

An Old Steel Engraving

Look.
The figure in the foreground breaks his fall with
one hand. He cannot die.
The river cannot wander
into the shadows to be dragged by willows.
The passer-by is scared witless. He cannot escape.
He cannot stop staring at
this hand which can barely raise
the patriot
above the ground which is
the origin and reason for it all.

More closely now:
at the stillness of unfinished action in
afternoon heat, at the spaces on the page. They widen
to include us:
we have found

the country of our malediction where
nothing can move until we find the word,
nothing can stir until we say this is

what happened and is happening and history
is one of us who turns away
while the other is
turning the page.

Is this river which
moments ago must have flashed the morse
of a bayonet thrust. And is moving on.

IX

In Exile

The German girls who came to us that winter and
the winter after and who helped my mother fuel
the iron stove and arranged our clothes in wet
thicknesses on the wooden rail after tea was over,

spoke no English, understood no French. They were
sisters from a ruined city and they spoke rapidly
in their own tongue: syllables in which pain was
radical, integral; and with what sense of injury

the language angled for an unhurt kingdom – for
the rise, curve, kill and swift return to the wrist,
to the hood – I never knew. To me they were the sounds
of evening only, of the cold, of the Irish dark and

continuous with all such recurrences: the drizzle in
the lilac, the dusk always at the back door, like
the tinkers I was threatened with, the cat inching
closer to the fire with its screen of clothes, where

I am standing in the stone-flagged kitchen; there are
bleached rags, perhaps, and a pot of tea on the stove.
And I see myself, four years of age and looking up,
storing such music – guttural, hurt to the quick –

as I hear now, forty years on and far from where
I heard it first. Among these salt-boxes, marshes and
the glove-tanned colours of the sugar-maples, in
this New England town at the start of winter, I am

so much South of it: the soft wet, the light and
those early darks which strengthen the assassin's
hand; and hide the wound. Here, in this scalding air,
my speech will not heal. I do not want it to heal.

X

We are Always too Late

Memory
is in two parts.

First, the re-visiting:

the way even now I can see
those lovers at the café table. She is weeping.

It is New England, breakfast-time, winter. Behind her,
outside the picture window, is
a stand of white pines.

New snow falls and the old,
losing its balance in the branches,
showers down,
adding fractions to it. Then

the re-enactment. Always that.
I am getting up, pushing away
coffee. Always, I am going towards her.

The flush and scald is
to her forehead now, and back down to her neck.

I raise one hand. I am pointing to
those trees, I am showing her our need for these
beautiful upstagings of
what we suffer by
what survives. And she never even sees me.

XI

What we Lost

It is a winter afternoon.
The hills are frozen. Light is failing.
The distance is a crystal earshot.
A woman is mending linen in her kitchen.

She is a countrywoman.
Behind her cupboard doors she hangs sprigged,
stove-dried lavender in muslin.
Her letters and mementoes and memories

are packeted in satin at the back with
gaberdine and worsted and
the cambric she has made into bodices;
the good tobacco silk for Sunday Mass.

She is sewing in the kitchen.
The sugar-feel of flax is in her hands.
Dusk. And the candles brought in then.
One by one. And the quiet sweat of wax.

There is a child at her side.
The tea is poured, the stitching put down.
The child grows still, sensing something of importance.
The woman settles and begins her story.

Believe it, what we lost is here in this room
on this veiled evening.
The woman finishes. The story ends.
The child, who is my mother, gets up, moves away.

In the winter air, unheard, unshared,
the moment happens, hangs fire, leads nowhere.
The light will fail and the room darken,
the child fall asleep and the story be forgotten.

The fields are dark already.
The frail connections have been made and are broken.
The dumb-show of legend has become language,
is becoming silence and who will know that once

words were possibilities and disappointments,
were scented closets filled with love-letters
and memories and lavender hemmed into muslin,
stored in sachets, aired in bed-linen;

and travelled silks and the tones of cotton
tautened into bodices, subtly shaped by breathing;
were the rooms of childhood with their griefless peace,
their hands and whispers, their candles weeping brightly?

XII

Outside History

There are outsiders, always. These stars –
these iron inklings of an Irish January,
whose light happened

thousands of years before
our pain did: they are, they have always been
outside history.

They keep their distance. Under them remains
a place where you found
you were human, and

a landscape in which you know you are mortal.
And a time to choose between them.
I have chosen:

out of myth into history I move to be
part of that ordeal
whose darkness is

only now reaching me from those fields,
those rivers, those roads clotted as
firmaments with the dead.

How slowly they die
as we kneel beside them, whisper in their ear.
And we are too late. We are always too late.

III

Distances

Exercises

Nights of Childhood

My mother kept a stockpot –

garlic cloves, bones,
rinds, pearl onions and the lacy spine and eyes
of a trout went into it.

When the window cleared, the garden showed
beyond the lemon balm,
through the steam,
cats.

Bucking. Rutting.
All buttocks and stripes.
Up on the wall and wild, they made the garden wild –
for all the gelded shrubs and the careful stemming
on trellises, of a bushed-out, pastel clematis.

One summer night I went out to them.
I looked up. Their eyes looked back –

not the colour of fields or kale,
the available greens,
but jade-cold
and with a closed-in chill I was used to –

lucid as a nursery rhyme and as hard to fathom,
revealed by rhythm, belied by theme
never forgotten

in those nights of childhood,
in a roomful of breathing, under wartime sheeting.

Outside, the screams and stridency of mating.

The Carousel in the Park

Find it.

Down the park walks, on the path leading
past the sycamores.
There through the trees –

nasturtium rumps, breasts plunging,
lime and violet manes
painted on
what was once the same as now littered
russet on their petrified advance.

Find the sun
in the morning rising later,
the chilled afternoons getting shorter and
after dusk, in the lake, in the park,
the downtown city windows scattering
a galaxy of money
in the water.

And winter coming:

the man-handled indigo necks flexing and
the flared noses
and the heads with their quiffed carving.

And the walks leafless and
the squirrels gone,
the sycamores bare and the lake frozen.

Find the child,
going high and descending there. Up and down.
Up, down again.
Her mittens bright as finger-paints and holding fast
to a crust of weather now: twelve years of age in
a thigh-length coat,
unable to explain a sense of ease in

those safe curves, that seasonless canter.

Contingencies

Waiting in the kitchen for power cuts,
on this wet night, sorting candles,
feeling the tallow,
brings back to me
the way women spoke in my childhood –

with a sweet mildness in front of company,
or with a private hunger in whispered kisses,
or with the crisis-bright words
which meant

you and you alone were their object –

'Stop that.' 'Wait till I get you.'
'Dry those tears.'

I stand the candles in jam jars
lined in a row on the table,
scalded and dried with a glass cloth;

which all last summer were crammed with
the fruits of neighbourly gardens.

Stoned plums and damsons. Loganberries.

Spring at the Edge of the Sonnet

Late March and I'm still lighting fires –

last night's frost which killed the new
shoots of ivy in the terracotta churn,
has turned the fields of wheat and winter barley

to icy slates on the hills rising
outside the windows of our living room.

Still, there are signs of change. Soon,
the roofs of cars, which last month were
oracles of ice and unthawed dawns,

will pass by, veiled in blooms from
the wild plum they parked under overnight.

Last night, as I drove from town,
the dark was in and the lovers were
out in doorways, using them as windbreaks,
making shadows seem nothing more than

sweet exchequers for a homeless kiss.

Our Origins are in the Sea

I live near the coast. On these summer nights
the dog-star rises somewhere near the hunter,
near the sun. I stand at the edge of our grass.

I do not connect them: once they were connected –
the fixity of stars and unruly salt water –
by sailors with an avarice for landfall.

And this is land. The way the whitebeams will
begin their fall to an alluvial earth and
a bicycle wheel is spinning on it, proves that.

From where I stand the sea is just a rumour.
The stars are put out by our streetlamp. Light
and seawater are well separated. And how little

survives of the sea-captain in his granddaughter
is everywhere apparent. Such things get lost:
He drowned in the Bay of Biscay. I never saw him.

I turn to go in. The hills are indistinct.
The coast is near and darkening. The stars are clearer.
The grass and the house are lapped in shadow.

And the briar rose is rigged in the twilight,
the way I imagine sails used to be –
lacy and stiff together, a frigate of ivory.

Midnight Flowers

I go down step by step.
The house is quiet, full of trapped heat and sleep.
In the kitchen everything is still.
Nothing is distinct; there is no moon to speak of.

I could be undone every single day by
paradox or what they call in the countryside
blackthorn winter,
when hailstones come with the first apple blossom.

I turn a switch and the garden grows.
A whole summer's work in one instant!
I press my face to the glass. I can see
shadows of lilac, of fuchsia; a dark likeness of blackcurrant:

little clients of suddenness, how sullen they are at
the margins of the light.
They need no rain, they have no roots.
I reach out a hand; they are gone.

When I was a child a snapdragon was
held an inch from my face. Look, a voice said, this
is the colour of your hair. And there it was, my head,
a pliant jewel in the hands of someone else.

Doorstep Kisses

The white iron of the garden chair is
the only thing dusk makes clearer.

I have stumbled on
the last days of summer in the last hour of light.

If I stay here long enough I may become –
since everything else around me is –

the sum of small gestures, choices,
losses in the air so fractional
they could be

fragrances which just fell from it –

a musk of buddleia, perhaps, or this fuchsia
with the drip,
drip of whitby jet fringing
an old rose printed shawl I saw once

which swung out and over my shoulders,
flinging out its scent
of early chills and doorstep kisses.

A Different Light

Talking just like this late at night
all depends on a sense of mystery;
the same things in a different light.

Your whisky glass and the watercolour
just off-centre are
part of this. The electric pallor

of that apple, also. And the slow
arc of an indoor palm, the vase beside it blooming
with shadows. Do you remember how

the power cuts caught us unawares?
No candles and no torch. It was high
summer. A soft brightness clung in the poplars,

for hours it seemed. When it went out,
everything we knew how
to look for had disappeared. And when light

came back, it came back as noise:
the radio; the deep freeze singing.
Afterwards we talked of it for days –

how it felt at the upstairs window,
to stand and watch and still miss the moment
of gable ends and rooftops beginning

to be re-built. And that split second when
you and I were, from a distance,
a neighbourhood on the verge of definition.

Hanging Curtains with an Abstract Pattern in a Child's Room

I chose these for you –
not the precinct of the unicorn, nor

the half-torn
singlet of a nursery rhyme prince, but

the signals of enigma:
Ellipse. Triangle. A music of ratio.

Draw these lines
against a winter dusk. Let them stand in for

frost on the spider's web and on
bicycle sheds.

Observe
how the season enters pure line

like a soul: all the signs we know
are only ways

of coming to our senses.
I can see

the distances off-loading colour now
into angles as

I hang their weather in
your room, all the time wondering

just how I look from the road –
my blouse off-white and

my skirt the colour of
all the disappointments of a day when

the curtains are pulled back on
a dull morning.

Ghost Stories

Our American Hallowe'en was years ago. We wore
anoraks and gloves
and stood outside to watch

the moon above Iowa. Before dark,
I walked out

through the parking lot and playground
to our apartment block.

On every porch, every doorstep, candles fluttered in
pumpkins in the dusk on the eve
of the holiday. We

were strangers
there. I remember how our lighted rooms
looked through curtains from the road:

with that fragility.

What Love Intended

I can imagine if,
I came back again,
    looking through windows at

broken mirrors, pictures,
and, in the cracked upstairs,
    the beds where it all began.

The suburb in the rain
this October morning,
    full of food and children

and animals, will be –
when I come back again –
    gone to rack and ruin.

I will be its ghost,
its revenant, discovering
    again in one place

the history of my pain,
my ordeal, my grace,
    unable to resist

seeing what is past,
judging what has ended
    and whether, first to last,

from then to now and even
here, ruined, this
    is what love intended –

finding even the yellow
jasmine in the dusk,
    the smell of early dinners,

the voices of our children,
taking turns and quarrelling,
burned on the distance,

gone. And the small square
where under cropped lime
and poplar, on bicycles

and skates in the summer,
they played until dark;
propitiating time.

And even the two whitebeams
outside the house gone, with
the next-door-neighbour

who used to say in April –
when one was slow to bloom –
they were a man and woman.

Distances

The radio is playing downstairs in the kitchen.
The clock says eight and the light says
winter. You are pulling up your hood against a bad morning.

Don't leave, I say. Don't go without telling me
the name of that song. You call it back to me from the stairs:
'I Wish I Was In Carrickfergus'

and the words open out with emigrant grief the way the streets
of a small town open out in
memory: salt-loving fuchsias to one side and

a market in full swing on the other with
linen for sale and tacky apples and a glass and wire hill
of spectacles on a metal tray. The front door bangs

and you're gone. I will think of it all morning while a fine
drizzle closes in, making the distances
fiction: not of that place but this and of how

restless we would be, you and I, inside the perfect
music of that basalt and sandstone
coastal town. We would walk the streets in

the scentless afternoon of a ballad measure,
longing to be able
to tell each other that the starched lace and linen of

adult handkerchiefs scraped your face and left your tears
falling; how the apples were mush inside the crisp sugar
shell and the spectacles out of focus.